a word of caution

This journal is meant to act as a catalyst for introspection. The deeper you can make yourself go, the deeper you can heal. Answer the prompt and then reflect by asking the "why's" until you gain a deeper understanding of who you really are and how your experiences have impacted your life. You can't hide from yourself and why would you want to. Integrate the darkness to become fully whole.

If you feel mentally fragile put this on the shelf until you are ready. Everything happens in the time it is meant to.

what is the darkest thought you've had?

how do you manipulate people?

who are you jealous of?

what do you hate about yourself?

what do you hate about your partner?

what's something illegal you would do if
you could get away with it?

What's the grossest thing you do when
no one is around?

what's the weirdest thing about you?

what makes you feel most like a failure?

what's your biggest regret?

what's your biggest regret?

what's the worst way you have betrayed someone?

when were you the most afraid?

what would people think if they knew the real you?

who have you let down the most?

what's something negative people think about you that's actually true?

why don't you think you're good enough?

how do you escape the reality of your life?

what's the biggest lie you tell yourself?

what are you addicted to?

what is the most painful thing you have
ever done to someone else?

what is the most painful thing you have
ever done to yourself?

what is your greatest fear?

what is your greatest fear?

what do you feel the most shameful about?

what was your most significant loss?

what trauma have you experienced?

who can't you ever forgive?

what has been your greatest sacrifice?

what has been your greatest lesson?

why do you need external validation?

what has hurt you the most?

why are you afraid to be your true self?

what are you most fearful of?

what has ever made you feel worthless?

what is your purpose in life?

what boundary do you allow people to cross most?

who broke your heart?

who's heart did you break?

what is your favorite childhood memory?

what is your worse childhood memory?

who loves you more than anyone else?

who do you love more than anyone else?

what is the greatest risk you've ever taken?

what is your biggest mistake?

what have you done that made you question your morals?

what do you need to change about yourself or your
life right now?

what is the worst thing you've ever done to get something you wanted?

what experiences have you buried so you don't have
to face them?

How have you sabotaged your own happiness?

How do you feel about your parents?

How do you feel about your children or extended
family if you don't have children?

____

____

____

____

____

____

____

____

____

____

____

____

How does being honest with yourself make you feel?

what are you most afraid of?

You did it! Hey... did you just skip to the back page? I hope you answered every question and kept it real with yourself. The only way out is through.

And yes, there were several prompts related to fear. There's a reason. Fear fosters the ego and the ego fosters fear. Tell both of them to kiss your ass.

I'm proud of you.